Note to Self

Homeless Single Mum to Six-Figure Income

Note to Self

Homeless Single Mum to Six-Figure Income

TATIANA SHARPOSHNIKOVA

Text Tatiana Sharposhnikova
Copyright © Tatiana Sharposhnikova

First print August 2023

CONTENTS

PROLOGUE	9
1. THE BEGINNING OF THE END	13
2. EXPECTATION HANGOVER	17
3. DON'T TELL ME I CAN'T AS I JUST MIGHT	23
4. THE CALL THAT SPLIT MY LIFE IRREVOCABLY INTO BEFORE AND AFTER	29
5. A RABBIT CAUGHT IN THE HEADLIGHTS	33
6. 'I'VE COME, MAMA. I'M HERE'	39
7. WHAT ALL GREAT SUCCESS STORIES HAVE IN COMMON	45
8. SUCCESS IS JUST 20 SECONDS AWAY	49
9. BUILDING SOMETHING OF VALUE AND GETTING IT RIGHT	59

10. THE PRICE I'VE PAID FOR SUCCESS	65
11. WHAT NEXT, TATIANA?	69
DEDICATION	75

PROLOGUE

When I came to England in October 1993, I was no more than a very naïve, unsuspecting Russian girl. I had no experience of the West, less still of a down-at-heel English seaside town in Kent, my unlikely destination in the UK. Not only could I not have imagined coming to England a few years before, I had never wanted to. As a child, I lived a sheltered life, adored by my father, and was a goody-two-shoes at school, a pretty ordinary teenager with few worries. Luck was also on my side when I set up a small business in Moscow, a convenience shop, which brought me a steady income. Meeting an English man and moving to the UK was certainly not on my agenda. And yet, I met my husband, an English man, and quickly forgot that life before him ever existed. Everything about him fascinated me – he was, in my eyes, this perfect English gentleman, full of knowledge and stories and experiences that were from a world I knew nothing about, a world that was full of colour, excitement, and opportunities. Though my English was very limited, and his Russian was non-existent, somehow, we never stopped talking whenever we met. Sure enough, soon we were living together in a rented flat in the centre of Moscow.

From the start in Moscow and for the following years of our lives together in the UK, I accepted everything he said and did without question. I saw him as my best friend, my confidant, my husband, my everything, especially during my first years in the UK, when I was dealing with overwhelming feelings of homesickness and isolation living in the country I neither knew nor understood. Six years into our lives in the UK, I was now a wife and a mum to our five-year-old son. I was also a university student studying international law, the first to do so in my family.

For this reason, the shock of what was to happen was immeasurable. I did not expect it, and nor was I prepared for it. I suspected nothing and was completely blindsided, ambushed by what life had in store for me. One sunny afternoon at the end of August 2000, my husband went on a business trip to Eastern Europe for a week and just disappeared. Days were followed by weeks, with nothing, not a word, no information – he had vanished without a trace. A couple of months later, I would get the news about what had happened to him from a total stranger, but it provided little comfort. Overnight, my life changed forever. From a quiet, suburban family life, I was to become a homeless, single mum with no means to live. The next few years would become a challenge and the fight of my life – my battle for survival.

Mine is a story of betrayal and abandonment, dark loneliness, the physical and emotional struggles of a young woman fighting for survival in a foreign country, the never-ending guilt of a working single parent, years of poverty, personal grief and emotional trauma.

NOTE TO SELF

Mine is also a story of hope and finding the strength to carry on in the darkest moments when it feels like the world is on your shoulders and there is no one to tell you that it will be OK. Through adversities and despair, I have never lost faith because in my heart, I have always known that I could use the determination my parents instilled in me to survive and improve my lot, and I have known the compassion of a few people along the way.

Ultimately, it is not a country or government that makes the difference between success and despair. It is we who determine and decide what happens next in our lives. Though we may not be able to choose the actions of others, we have the power to define our responses to what happens to us in life and to the events by which we have no control. Moving to England from Russia was not the secret to my happily ever after. In fact, the first few years in the UK were the most traumatic times of my life, even to this day, having lived here for over twenty years, but they were also the making of me.

Fast-forward twenty years. I now own and manage several businesses, all relating to real estate. I had also set up and managing a legal practice, RSL-LAW, a well-known law firm in central London, specialising in property law. We celebrated twelve years in business this year, and despite Brexit and Covid with all the consequential lockdowns and recent political unrest, my boutique legal practice has reached a turnover at the high end of six-figure income.

NOTE TO SELF

The lessons I learned in business were invaluable. I wish ME now could give advice and guidance to ME then; we would have probably achieved our current success a lot earlier. I will share these lessons with you.

I fought and survived, often one step at a time, finding my way from abandonment and isolation to emotional well-being again, forging my path in business. My determination made the difference between despair and survival. Unfortunately, it took me a very long time to learn that equally important is the mindset and conscious decision of choosing to be OK, to be strong and positive, and not to allow yourself to drown in your self-pity or let others drag you down with them. I could have saved myself so much emotional pain along the way.

Having been through so much, then emerging on the other side with different values, better than ever, happy and successful, I hope my story will help those who have lost hope, who feel all alone right now, who see no way out and have nowhere to turn; it will get better – it always does – it did for me, and it will for you.

1. THE BEGINNING OF THE END

It was an especially hot August afternoon, as I sat in the waiting room of the local Jobcentre, listening for my name to be called out. My eyes darted from one person to another. I felt, and no doubt looked, frightened, lost, desperate, and completely alone. I was a rabbit caught in the headlights, with a lorry hurtling towards me.

The room was cacophonous, a riot of talking and shouting. Men laughed raucously, cradling beer cans in their hands. Mothers snapped at their children, who circled in a welter of cries and screeches. Just as appalling as the noise was the suffocating smell of the room and the dulling discomfort of the hard, plastic chair digging into the back of my thighs. It was all so alien – here I was, homeless, utterly alone, and completely lost. Mere weeks earlier, I'd had a comfortable house, a husband and a place at university whilst being a mother to my son. The contrast was shocking, unbelievable. How could this have happened to my father's daughter, of whom he was so proud, the first in the family to go to university, his little girl married to an 'English gentleman'? I was supposed to be living the good life, loved and protected, but instead, it was my childhood in Russia that had given me protection – the love of my parents, the respect of my friends, the success of my own business, the security of my apartment in Moscow. Then, I had not had a worry in the world; now, fear and panic overcame me.

There I sat, waiting in that terrible room, thoughts pounding in my head. I was about to be homeless, with no money, no husband, and my five-year-old son unreachable in Moscow. Round and round went the panic and terror as I contemplated what to do next. The landlord of the house that we could no longer afford to rent had suggested that the Jobcentre might provide me with some direction, so there I sat, endlessly waiting, waiting, hoping against hope that some guardian angel might come to my aid.

'Tatiana?', a plump lady with grey hair in an oversized jumper called out into the room. I jumped at the sound of my name voiced above the surrounding din and walked to the booth, where another woman sat on the far side of the plastic screen. Her kind eyes, nestled in her careworn face, struck me instantly. Something told me that she, perhaps my only 'friend' then, would help me. This unknown human being might provide some hope of rescue. She looked down at some yellow forms lying on her desk, pushed her glasses up to the top of her nose, looked at me, then down again, and finally asked in a steady, neutral voice, 'Full name?'

'Tatiana,' I said, feeling the tears welling up, the tears of the continued raw shock and disbelief at how my life had, in mere weeks, become entirely unrecognisable. I sank into a

NOTE TO SELF

reverie; I could see her lips moving, but I could not hear her words. I stared back listlessly for what felt like an eternity.

'Surname?' the kind-eyed woman asked. I looked at her, then at the waiting room, and back at her again and suddenly burst into uncontrollable tears. Once I had started, I could not stop. Try as I might, uttering my surname was beyond me, as my whole body wracked and heaved with sobs of despair. The noise seemed to evaporate as my consciousness seemed reduced only to that miserable, wretched sobbing.

I desperately wanted to tell her that my husband of six years had told me he was going away on a business trip for a week and disappeared without a trace. Gone, vanished, out of reach, now a figment of my imagination, and I had no idea where he was or how to find him. I wanted to explain that I was being evicted from my home because he had left the rent unpaid for months, that my son was stranded miles away in Moscow with his grandparents as I had no means of picking him up; he needed to start school in a few weeks, and I had no more than £5 between me and penury. I was broke, finished, at the end of the road. I yearned to confide in her as I would have confided in my parents had they been there to say that I had no idea what to do or how to emerge from this hideous mess. I craved her help. But all I could do was cry and cry some more.

Above the tumult of the room and the sound of my own tears, I heard the kind lady shouting to her left, 'This one's for the blue room!' Then, an escort guided me through the 'Staff Only' door to a room with blue walls, where I heard myself say for the first time aloud, 'I have been abandoned, I have nowhere to live, and I don't know what to do.'

It was August 2000 when my life was split irrevocably into 'before' and 'after'.

Note to Self:
Sometimes, the circumstances are much bigger than us, and it's OK to feel helpless, lost, and even desperate. It will pass; there will be another day, a better day, guaranteed! All you need to do is reach out, ask for help, and not be alone. Sometimes, all it takes is not being alone.

2. EXPECTATION HANGOVER

When I came to England, I had no experience of the West at all, and the furthest foreign destination I had ever travelled to without my parents was Poland – and even then, it was with a group of friends. A few months earlier, I had met an Englishman – I will call him 'H' – who was frequently in Moscow on business. We had several dates, and he returned to England. I thought that would be it, and I would continue my busy life in Moscow, studying English and running my own small business, a retail kiosk. There were many of these kiosks all over the city, a sign of newly found freedom for entrepreneurs at the time. I had not anticipated living in the UK, and nor had I ever wanted to.

I had a very happy childhood, and though we did not have much money, love and laughter were abundant. My teenage years followed in the same vein, so when I became a young woman, I was well-settled and happy and had no desire to leave my country. To my surprise, H came back to Moscow a month later. Within another month, I moved into a flat he rented in the city centre, close to the Arbat, the historic heart of Moscow. Life continued – apparently – as usual. H raised the subject of me going with him to England numerous times, but I said I would only consider it for a short visit; moving

NOTE TO SELF

away from my parents and everything else I knew and loved seemed too scary.

I felt this way until one afternoon in October 1993. We were on a stroll, approaching the city centre, when I noticed it was surprisingly busy – many people were out on the streets. Suddenly, we saw people running, some purposefully and some in panic. The White House (Russian Federation Government House) was visible in front of us, and to my horror, I saw tanks and soldiers with full ammunition holding their guns in the 'ready' position. A few minutes later, we heard gunfire, loud and fast and very close, which sounded as if it was going over the top of our heads. Everyone started running in different directions, and we found ourselves, as we knew later, in the middle of the 1993 October Coup – the confrontation between the Russian president, Boris Yeltsin, and a few members of the Russian parliament who were calling for his impeachment, disagreeing with his governing policies.

The rebellious members of the parliament locked themselves in the White House, accompanied by supporters fully equipped with machine guns and ammunition. They had been occupying the White House for over a week, protecting their positions with gunfire aimed at everyone and anyone approaching the White House. That afternoon, demonstrators who wanted to see Yeltsin back in the White House stormed the building at his command with the help of the army, arresting the leaders of the resistance. The 10-day

NOTE TO SELF

conflict ended with hundreds of people killed; this was the 1993 October Coup, now known as Black October.

Running away from the gunfire, bullets whistling inches away from our ears, made me think that there must be a better way to live, a better place to raise a family. That evening, I agreed to go to England with H.

We planned to travel around England for a while to see how I liked it before deciding what to do next and where we would want to live. By then, we had decided we wanted to be together and start a family. I said my goodbyes to my papa and had my mama see me off at the Sheremetyevo airport. It was a big deal, a big family event – I was leaving Russia to start my new life with my English husband. I did not know then, standing at the airport, saying goodbye to my mama, that the next time I would see her and my dad would be several years later and that I would be an unrecognisable mess. A shadow of myself, emotionally broken and completely alone, facing the fight of my life for survival for myself and my son, who at that time was yet to be born.

Even at the start, the experience was a shock to the system. I, a one hundred percent, city-oriented Muscovite girl who had enjoyed a happy childhood, strong friendships, a vibrant social life, and a comfortable lifestyle, found myself in the colonial backwater that was my new home, a little seaside town in Kent. My husband's hometown was a far cry from what I had heard about London. Instead of the energy of one of the world's leading capital cities, I catapulted into an eerily

NOTE TO SELF

quiet, strange town dominated by the retired population, where I felt entirely cut off from any community it might have had.

Worse, we had no home and spent the first month living in a cheap hotel before we moved into a rented flat. When I asked H what had happened to his 'beautiful apartment' he had told me so much about back in Moscow, describing it in detail as his classy bachelor pad, he explained there was a burglary just before we arrived and that the burglars had left such a mess, that he did not want to go back there and certainly did not want to take me there. Though it did sound extreme and quite dramatic, I believed him unquestioningly. I had no grasp on our situation and looked to H as my friend, guide and husband – he was my everything. That made me vulnerable. With no understanding of how our life operated or the dynamics of the English existence, I was entirely reliant on H and his protection. I was now living in a country I could not understand. I had only studied English for a few months before arrival, so my linguistic abilities were poor. How could I hope to appreciate a country where everything was different, from the obvious things – the language, the people, their reserved English manner – to the extraordinarily barren streets after 6:30 in the evening when the small seaside town seemed to die, becoming empty and almost ethereal? Having been a ball of energy, constantly abuzz with business or learning, family, and friends, I was suddenly in this flat, sitting by the window, watching a few cars driving past, now pregnant.

NOTE TO SELF

England was a country with a different pulse that was a more formal and colder than my own. It was almost another planet and a shock to the system for me. Especially during my first few years, I could sense prejudice against me. Whether it was just the mindset of small-town people or the time we lived in, many assumed I was a 'Russian bride' coming to the UK for a better life, escaping the poverty of my homeland. I would learn to brush off such attitudes and rude corrections of my English, sometimes from complete strangers, but they still stung.

I would often think, 'What am I doing here? I don't belong here.' I missed my parents constantly and was extremely homesick. My life then was a far cry from the shelter my parents had always provided. In Russia, family ties are strong. My husband's family was quite the opposite. Visits to his parents' house for Sunday lunch constituted a formal event, carefully arranged and organised well in advance. It was a big difference from a typical Moscow apartment where two generations would often live side by side, involved in each other's lives.

The start of my new foreign life, which I had imagined would be bright and compelling with so many new adventures, was, in fact, the most confusing, isolating, and sombre experience. What I did not know at the time was that it was about to get much worse.

NOTE TO SELF

Note to Self:
If you sense that you are being lied to, perhaps you are. We all have an 'internal compass' that signals truth or fiction, peace or trouble. Trust that. If you sense someone is lying to you, don't agree or nod or laugh in reply; don't allow that person to feel comfortable about doing it. It will not get better, but you will learn to live with it. You deserve so much better.

3. DON'T TELL ME I CAN'T AS I JUST MIGHT

I am inclined to take people at face value, so when my relationship with H developed, it did not occur to me to think that he was anything other than single. I knew he had been married and had a son with his ex-wife. I just assumed that he was divorced. My mother was similarly accepting and was content for me to come to England. My father was more reserved, concerned that things might not work out and only giving me his blessing when I acquired an open ticket so I could return to Moscow, if need be, at any time in the next twelve months.

But once my son was born there was no question of returning. I remember that time well. I would wander around the deserted streets of my little seaside town with him in a pram, window shopping or taking refuge by the beach, sitting on a bench whilst he slept next to me. Sometimes, I would not speak to another adult all day, as H was out meeting business associates – or so he said. Then one day, I saw two ladies who looked like a mother and daughter, who stood out from the usual 'small-town' people. Then I detected them speaking Russian. I was so desperate to hear the language spoken again that I caught up to them and said: 'Zdravstvuite!' Or 'hello' in Russian.

NOTE TO SELF

We spoke for a few minutes, and I immediately invited them to our house. We drank tea with fresh lemon and chatted about anything and everything. I was happy for the first time in a long while. In time, I would meet a few more Russian-speaking friends, but they could not alleviate the strain of communication with my husband. I remained in a culture shock, with no support network and my family many tortuous miles away.

I might have been living in a beautiful house by then, but I could not adapt to the somewhat cold reserve of the English, which stood in such stark contrast to the emotional directness of Russians. On rare occasions, when we visited H's friends for a Sunday barbecue, I was the odd one out. Curious glances, jokes (apparently in good humour) about my pronunciation of some English words and whispers about me and where I came from as if I was not there, became all too familiar. At the time, I just brushed them off.

The small-mindedness of this seaside cul-de-sac fuelled a deep unease inside me. Eventually, I realised I was desperately missing the person I had been in Moscow. I needed to do something, but my English remained broken, and every conversation I started with H on the subject always ended with: 'You can't do it. You need money to study', or 'It will take you years', or 'Who will look after the house?'.

NOTE TO SELF

I would usually admit defeat and force the thought to the back of my mind. That was until one sunny afternoon – I pushed my son's pram along a leafy street as I passed big black gates, a red-brick building, a football pitch and tennis courts behind them. A minute later, I saw a sign that read 'Kent College'. Curiosity got the better of me, and I turned into the gates, my son happily snoozing in his pram. As I walked through the doors, I saw a reception desk in front of me, with a young lady behind it. She was wearing trendy glasses and looked well-dressed. Seeing her made me remember how much I missed my old Russian life. I had no idea what I was doing there or what I wanted to ask her. Part of me just wanted to talk, as was often the case – striking up conversations with café owners and sales assistants was becoming a bit of a routine in my effort to feel less isolated. The trendy lady gave me a friendly smile. 'Hi there. How can I help?'

'I would like to study, but I'm not sure what I want to do. I don't speak English very well, but I do speak Russian', I said in my broken English. She reached over to her left, picked up some leaflets, and handed them to me. 'You can see all the courses here. Since you speak a second language, you could get a job in London – many companies there employ people who speak different languages.'

One of the booklets had a list of different courses. *Foundation Course for Legal Studies* jumped off the page. 'What job can I do if I take this?'

NOTE TO SELF

She explained that I could go on to take a secretarial course and become a legal secretary, a highly sought-after role in London, particularly amongst international law firms. I was immediately excited, particularly about the 'international law firms' part, thinking, only two years, and then I could join one of these companies, earning my own money, and above all, I could be in an environment of like-minded people – the intellectual and cultural life I was yearning.

'What about a lawyer? How long would I need to study to become a lawyer?' I mused, immediately feeling a buzz of excitement at the enormity of the challenge the idea represented to me at the time. After all, I could scarcely speak English, and her expression was incredulous. Should someone who articulated such bad English be contemplating such a thing? She replied – not without derision – that following the foundation course the college offered (1 year), I would need a law degree (three years), then go to law school (a further year) and complete a training contract - working in a law firm for two years under the supervision of a qualified lawyer (another two years). When she told me that it would be very competitive, verging on the impossible, I decided that it was exactly what I wanted to do.

As with pretty much everything in my life, from then until this day, I am always exhilarated by a new challenge. I want to be the best at whatever I do; I want it all, and I am prepared to do what it takes. So it was with my university course. The European legal studies course was not a conventional three-year law degree but a four-year course requiring students to spend their third year abroad in either Sweden or the Netherlands, studying European and international law. That presented a conundrum, as I had a young son and a husband. What was I thinking? Who was I to study in Europe? That was the privilege of the rich kids. But my heart, my ambition and my drive were saying the opposite. I wanted this opportunity so much; it was the opportunity of a lifetime for me.

I could not help myself – I made that all-important call to my mother in Moscow, asking if she would come to stay with me. 'It will only be for a few months, and I will be coming back every few weeks, as Maastricht is only a few hours away'. To my surprise, H, who was planning a busy few months himself, was not against it either.

The time then came for me to go to Holland. My mother, a devoted Russian mum who only wanted what was best for her daughter, came to England to look after her grandson. H was also busy, constantly on business trips whilst I was studying most of the time and travelling back home every few weeks to see the family. Things had some order. By the end of the school year and my time in Maastricht, my mother returned home, taking her grandson with her to visit his grandpa Victor and his cousins. A week later, I was returning from Maastricht to meet H at our house, as we had agreed to spend a couple of weeks together before flying to Moscow to pick up our son. I was looking forward to seeing him, to the Moscow trip, to coming back home to the UK, to my last academic year at university, and to settling back into the routine of our family life. But things would turn out quite differently . . .

Note to Self:
Your family and friends should be your biggest supporters. You shouldn't feel guilty for wanting to better yourself, to grow as a person. You will only be as good as the people you surround yourself with. So, if you find yourself surrounded by people who make you doubt yourself, question your self-esteem, tell you that you can't do what you want to do for a million reasons, make you feel down and unloved, it's better to be alone. It is never too late to be what you might have been.

4. THE CALL THAT SPLIT MY LIFE IRREVOCABLY INTO BEFORE AND AFTER

Arriving home from Holland, full of anticipation at seeing H and going to Russia, I found the house locked. Inside, it was eerily cold. Mouldy tea stood in a rancid cup on the kitchen table. Nobody was at home. Nobody had been at home for some time, perhaps ever since my mother had left a few weeks ago. I hastily walked around the rooms, looking into each one and expecting to see H, or even something – a note, a letter – anything that would explain the empty house.

My mind raced. The last time I saw H was on my last weekend home. We had chatted, laughed and made plans whilst he packed a small travel bag for a weeklong business trip to Slovakia. I wandered around the house disconsolately, each room more freezing than the last. What was going on? I tried to call him several times – no answer. In a vacuum of information, I was confused, terrified, and at a loss as to what was happening and what I should do. Tired and confused, I fell asleep. I woke up the next day, the next, and the day after that to the same empty house and non-existent answers.

NOTE TO SELF

After a week of barely functioning and trying to understand what I should do next, there was a knock at the door. The landlord wanted to see H. For the first time, I found myself saying aloud to another person that I neither knew where my husband was nor what was happening. That's when the landlord dealt the second major blow: 'Your husband has failed to pay rent for three months now. I tried to contact him, but he won't answer. I am afraid you need to leave'. I had no more than a month at the most; we were facing eviction. I felt completely numb, with no food in the house, my credit card maxed to the limit, and no money except for a few pounds in coins left loose on the worktop in the kitchen.

Another week had passed, I barely ate or slept, as I tried to compose myself and figure out my next step, the phone rang; I knew it was H – it had to be. He would explain everything. There would be a simple explanation for this. 'Hi, Tatiana?' a woman's voice said at the other end. 'You probably don't remember me, but you came to our house for a barbecue. Your husband is a friend of my husband'. I listened in silence, confused, my heart pounding.

'Look, if anyone asks, I didn't call you, and I will deny everything'. She paused. 'But I felt you should know he stayed at our house last weekend'. My mind raced. What was she saying? What did she mean by 'last weekend'? He was here, in town, last weekend? Somehow it made me feel happy and hopeful. But wait, why had he not come home? Why was he not answering his phone? The voice on the phone waited for a

NOTE TO SELF

few seconds, then said, 'He won't be coming home. He has another family in Slovakia. The woman he is living with over there is eight months pregnant'. Again, she paused, 'I'm sorry. Best of luck'. She hung up. I stood there for what felt like an eternity, holding the phone to my ear.

I remember my vision going in and out of focus, my mind grappling with this information. I felt as if I was in a film, that what this woman said had nothing to do with me. That moment was utterly surreal. The woman gave me his new mobile number, which, when I rang, was answered immediately. He wasn't expecting it to be me. Against the backdrop of restaurant noises, I said to him, overcome by his voice, 'You're alive! What's happening? Where are you?'

I could sense that he was shocked to hear from me; he mumbled something inaudible, then snapped that he couldn't talk and would call me later and hung up. I rang him again – I must have called him back more than ten times in total, in sheer panic, but his phone was now off.

That was when I called my mother, standing in the middle of the sitting room of a very cold house, about to be homeless, feeling as through a train had hit me. As soon as I heard her voice, I burst into a torrent of tears. 'Please . . . ' she said, 'Tell me you have someone there, a friend or a neighbour; anyone. Please don't be alone right now'. She started crying. But there was no one. I was alone. There was no coming back from this. My life was about to change forever.

NOTE TO SELF

Note to Self:
Betrayal. It never comes from your enemies; it never comes expected. And the worst thing about betrayal is that it can destroy you if you let it. It takes one person, weak and selfish, to betray and another, strong and proud, to survive.

5. A RABBIT CAUGHT IN THE HEADLIGHTS

'This one's for the blue room!' The phrase repeated itself in my head as I stepped into the room. As well as the blue walls, I noticed a flickering, fluorescent light making a simultaneous clicking noise. The room itself smelt of old furniture and a hot, sweaty August day. A woman invited me to sit, pointing to a stool opposite the desk. 'I have been abandoned, I have nowhere to live, and I don't know what to do.' I mumbled through tears, pleading silently for the woman to make it all OK, to make it all go away.

It did not take long to tell her what had happened – after all, the story was short. I told her how the happily-ever-after had crashed to a halt when my husband left the country to live with another woman who was about to give birth to their child. Coincidentally, I explained, I was a student, had nowhere to live and no money to live on and needed to get my son back from Russia somehow, to have him ready for school. She was very sympathetic and offered to add me to the waiting list for free accommodation, which I would get in a couple of months. It was hopeless.

Having experienced the depths of humiliation and despair of the 'blue room' as a homeless, penniless mother, I realised that my back was to the wall. Going back to Russia was not an option – my parents had divorced years earlier and lived in small apartments with their new spouses. And in any case, coming to England had been my idea, my risk, so I was not willing to go home with my tail between my legs and become a burden to my parents. I had to sort things out myself.

I rang my father, who agreed to send me some money he had saved over the years, so I could fly to Moscow to pick up my little boy. As I landed at Sheremetyevo Airport, the flood of old memories made me shake uncontrollably, tears pouring down my cheeks. Just seven years ago, I had stood here full of hope, in love, excited, waving my mother goodbye on my way to London. It wasn't a happy trip.

When we got back to the UK, I scraped together a small deposit, to rent a tiny basement flat on the border of the 'right side' of town. I vividly remember the sense of utter uncertainty as I explained to my son that, from now on, there would be just the two of us – him and me. At six years old, it was too much for him to understand; he seemed as happy as ever. I, on the contrary, understood that there was no more room for me or my emotions. I had to shut down. I had to grow up. I had to accept the challenge of being a single mother, a provider for my child, and a student.

After lots of discussions, my father and I decided that I must finish my degree. But it would take me a year with only the pitiful student grant to subsidise us, so I knew it would be tough. We survived in our tiny basement flat, which had not so much as a fridge, intermittent electricity, and an emotionally unstable neighbour screaming the building down whenever he argued with his girlfriend – a daily occurrence.

That year was awful, an endurance test of grinding poverty. The sense of isolation was absolute – there was no chance for me to make friends at university; most students lived on campus and focused on having a good time and going out, whilst I was a single mother with no money. After lectures, I had to race back in my little old car to pick my son up from a neighbour, as I could not afford childcare. Once, I ran to the car park to find that my car would not start. I kept turning the key in the ignition but to no avail. I burst into tears, knowing that no one would pick my baby boy up if I did not. I was alone, and I was responsible for everything. It was up to me to ensure we functioned and survived, and the car would not start. I remember this odd story because, to this day, I can see the faces of a couple of people in the car park, looking at me in bemusement. It probably seemed such an overreaction to them – it was just a car. It was not a big deal, so why on earth was this woman in such a state, crying and angry? It would be impossible for them to understand that this was a tragedy, that every little thing that went wrong in my life then was a tragedy, as every day, I had less and less emotional and physical capacity to deal with yet another misfortune.

The silver lining was that my son was at school, my studies were concluding, and I received an offer for a training contract with one of the top ten London law firms, who also paid for my year at the London Law School. I was now travelling to London every day. And though we had survived for over a year since H left, I was beginning to fully understand the pressures of being a single mum. I was forever stressed. Whilst everyone else went to coffee shops and cafés to discuss the day's lectures, I was always running out and racing to the train station to make the hour's journey back home to pick up my son. If I was not there to pick him up, nobody else would be. I could not miss the train. I could not afford to miss the train. The stress was interminable, such that people would look at me and say, 'Slow down!' as if nothing could possibly be that important to plunge me into a state of perpetual neurosis and anxiety.

Then one day, having picked my son up after another day at the law school and having made our way to our little basement flat, feeling utterly exhausted, I found a message on my answerphone from my cousin in Moscow. It had already been a gloomy day, encapsulated by the dismal, squelching noise my leaking left shoe had made as I rushed yet again to the station. I had meant to mend it for weeks but had no time nor money.

I was surprised to get a message from my cousin, as we were not close. Something told me I had to call her back. 'You need to come home,' she said, 'and you need to come home now'.

Note to Self:

Life never was intended to be easy. It is full of challenges, tests and burdens, personal or in your business life. When you are in the epicentre of a situation, clarity of mind and the talent of staying calm goes a long way to help you keep standing. And once you live through the challenges and survive them, you undoubtedly become a better person, capable of living a more fulfilling life.

Outrageous, extroverted, and always happy, thanks to the huge energy you had, one that I now share

6. 'I'VE COME, MAMA. I'M HERE'

'Allo?', my cousin's voice echoed on the other end of the phone, 'Your mum has only a few days left to live', silence, 'Are you there?'. I was there all right, holding onto the phone, but I could not speak nor understand what she was telling me. My cousin must have understood as much as she continued, 'She has cancer. She has been sick for a while, but she wouldn't let any of us call you. She had hidden your phone number under her pillow, knowing what you were going through lately. It was when she was out on morphine the other day that I got a hold of it. You must hurry! She is waiting for you. Tanya, you need to come now.'

The next day, I went to law school after dropping my son off. The conversation with my cousin the night before did not seem real. Of course, I knew I had not imagined it, but how could it be true? My mama had always been a glowing example of happiness – sporty, beautiful, smiley, and she was only fifty-nine. The news did not seem real. However, I did realise that I had to get to Moscow as quickly as possible. As soon as I got to law school, I went to see my tutor. It was not until I was sitting in front of him, that I realised I could not speak. I had the words in my head, but I could not say them aloud. I must have looked terrified as my tutor asked me if I was OK, visibly concerned.

NOTE TO SELF

'I have to go to Moscow. My mama is dying.'

I remember feeling every ounce of composure leave my body, tears running down my cheeks, getting into my mouth, and my nose running. I tried to say something else, to explain, but only incoherent things came out, as I choked on my sobs. My tutor was visibly shocked, offering me a box of tissues.

'Of course. I am so sorry to hear that. Don't you worry about anything, of course', he kept saying, but the words were not registering with me. I was in fear, disbelief and hysteria.

Things did not improve when my stepfather came to pick me up at the airport. The jolt of seeing someone who had looked after me since my early teens, who now shared with me a silent understanding of the reason for our meeting, was almost too much. He looked serious, and I, well, just terrified.

'How is she?' I asked him in the car. I will never forget the face that looked back at me: the face of total defeat, grief, and helplessness. 'She is going, but you will make it', he said, looking away at the car window, swallowing hard.

The drive took about twenty-five minutes. We were silent most of the way, afraid to speak, in shock. It was strange to recognise all the streets, the roads, the shops, the buildings – so familiar and friendly from my childhood, only now, I was terrified, and none of this made sense. As soon as the car pulled up at the block of flats by the entrance, I ran up the five flights of stairs. She lived on the top floor. The door to the apartment was unlocked, so I pushed it open and stepped in. An overwhelming smell of medication and cooking hit me. I passed through the corridor and the sitting room like a shadow, and there I was, just outside her bedroom, where I knew she was lying, my mama, lying and dying. Yet again, I had to be strong. I had to hold everyone and everything together. I quietly stepped in and saw her. The image will stay with me forever.

Her tiny body, the body of a woman I barely recognised, her head turned away from the bedroom door towards the window. She looked like a little girl, just skin and bones, huge dark eyes, frightened and moaning in pain. As she sensed me, she slowly turned her head towards the door, our eyes met, and she struggled into a smile. My heart was racing, and my mind was numb. A wave of heat and blind fear consumed me. I was, I now know, in total shock. I sat down on the edge of her bed.

'What have you done? Why didn't you ring me?'. She moved her skinny right hand towards mine, just our fingers touching. 'You came?' she whispered. 'I've come, Mama. I'm here', I whispered back, scooping her into my arms. I saw tears running down her cheeks. I wiped them with my hand. 'Stop it. Look what I brought you', I said, pulling out a picture of her grandson playing rugby and showing it to her. She looked at the photograph and wanted to say something, but the drugs she was on took over, and she lost consciousness.

NOTE TO SELF

I sat on the edge of her bed, touching her hand, watching her face, not crying, not talking, just watching her, her chest going up and down very slowly, in disbelief, shock and the cold realisation that the end was just hours away. It must have been around five in the morning when I dozed off by her side for a few minutes, waking up to a strange noise, hissing or snoring, before everything went quiet. Very quiet. My devoted mama, my giggly, happy, loud, kind and beautiful mama, died on 12th October 2001. We buried her next to my grandmother a couple of days later, and the next day, I left for the UK without fully realising what had just happened.

Back in England, I was living with anguish, a trauma I have never recovered from – yet another massive shock. My heart broke. I went from not knowing that my mother was even ill to losing her completely. I had no time to talk to her, to remember my childhood with her, to get used to the awfulness of her not being there anymore. Back in my basement flat, I just wanted to die – at least then, I could be with her again. At that point, I was close to a breakdown. They say you are only given as much misfortune as you can bear; at that point, I could not handle any more – the hardship of the last couple of years, the grief, the despair, the loneliness and darkness, nothing ahead, just darkness. But I had my son, looking at me, waiting to be fed and taken to the park and for his mama to take care of everything; to make it all better. I had no choice but to carry on. Just shut down again and carry on.

NOTE TO SELF

In Loving Memory:
Do not stand at my grave and weep. I am not there; I do not sleep. I am a thousand winds that blow; I am the diamond glints on snow; I am the sunlight on ripened grain; I am the gentle autumn rain. When you awaken in the morning's hush, I am the swift uplifting rush of quiet birds in circled flight. I am the soft stars that shine at night. Don't stand at my grave and cry. I am not there; I did not die.
Mary Elizabeth Frye

7. WHAT ALL GREAT SUCCESS STORIES HAVE IN COMMON

Strangely enough, for the first time since coming to England all that time ago in 1993, I felt almost at home here, certainly more at home than I was in my country of birth. The Moscow I had visited so briefly for a last glimpse of my mother and to attend her funeral was a totally different place from the city I had known. It was almost like another society. There were cafés and restaurants, shopping centres, very well-dressed people, expensive cars on the roads, fancy skyscraper offices, and residential estates. This Russia seemed foreign to me, and I certainly could not face starting all over again in a country I knew little about. Though England was not home either, I had nowhere to go and nowhere to be but England.

I began my training contract in September 2002, qualifying as an English solicitor in September 2004. I then took employment with a city law firm. It was a good experience for a couple of years, but I needed to explore other opportunities, and a few years later, I moved to a large US law firm and spent a few years practising law in London with occasional trips to their Moscow office. I loved and hated those trips.

I loved them because I always arranged to meet my papa somewhere in the city, not far from the hotels where I was staying. We would get lost wandering around the city centre, stopping for lunches somewhere quiet, and we would talk and talk and talk, reminiscing and catching up. He would often travel a long way from his country home back into the city to see me for an hour. The bond between us has always been unbreakable. However, those trips always took me away from home, away from my son, making me feel guilty every time; I hated them. Not only did I put myself under pressure to succeed in a male-dominated profession and a foreign country, but I was also constantly wracked with guilt so familiar to all single parents – the shame of not being home for school runs, sports days and bedtimes.

Generally, my life appeared to be in some order compared to my situation a few years earlier. That was wonderful, but even though my life sounded better than average, even glamorous at times with all those foreign trips, the truth was that I hated every minute of it; the snobby and standoffish attitude of some of my colleagues, constantly feeling as if I was looked down upon. Nothing was what it seemed; office politics at every level – partners, associates, secretaries. There were days when I would not say a single word to another person, sitting in my fancy office emailing or reading documents. There was no client contact, as that was for partners only. I felt like a fish out of water. I did not belong there. I was beginning to realise that the big-city corporate world might not be for me. I was too personable for it.

NOTE TO SELF

So after several years of being employed as a solicitor, I decided to go it alone. It was not that I knew anything about business or running a company, but, at the time, there was a clear gap in the market for legal advice and support for Russian-speaking clients in their language. The market was failing to meet the needs of the growing number of successful Russian businesspeople wanting to set up a business or buy property in the UK. Nobody was helping them, and they fell between the cracks of large, old-fashioned English law firms that might have a junior-associate Russian speaker at best and lesser, rural high-street firms with no cultural understanding of my country and how business works there; this presented an opportunity.

I knew this was going to be an uphill climb for me. As much as I now knew I hated the cold and impersonal corporate world, I lived in terror of not having a pay cheque. After all, my son and I only had one pay cheque, and it was mine. I was also terrified of escaping my mindset from my school years. If you study hard at school, you go to university, get a degree and a good job, get promoted, and get paid. You do not step outside the path expected and accepted by society. I had always been conscientious at school, had made a decent job of the opportunity to go to an international university, and had landed a series of promising legal jobs. Was I willing to forsake that for unknown gain? Well, yes, because I knew I had the ability and stamina to compete, to push myself, and to derive strength from the lessons of my upbringing. I had nothing to lose, no cherished fortune to squander. All the money I earned thus far, I spent on paying for our lives. I wanted to be free, my own boss, and above all, happy, to move beyond a rhythm of life that was starting to imprison me. But I had no idea how I was going to survive. I just knew I did not fit into English suburban life or emotionless corporate life; in fact, I did not fit in anywhere, so it was time to create my own space in the UK where I would fit in.

Note to Self:
If you are not happy, take a chance. Decide to jump into the unknown rather than simply carrying on with your life for another five or ten years as you have done for the last five or ten because it's safer, and less scary. All achievements and success stories have one simple yet powerful characteristic in common – the first step. Keep your day job for a short while if you must or learn to live on less money whilst pursuing what you always wanted to do. Don't let fear stop you, and every single reason 'why not' you are shouting at me right now – excuses! You obviously don't want it badly enough. Give yourself a chance to be great and to be happy. Take the first step, and the journey has a way of taking care of itself. If not now, when? And even if the new journey may not be the success you dream of, it will lead you to places and people that will change your life – guaranteed!

8. SUCCESS IS JUST 20 SECONDS AWAY

My legal practice was born, and I was taking baby steps with little idea of what I was doing. There was no clever marketing, analysis, or research – I did not know how to go about those, so mine was a DIY approach. I had a track record in the legal profession and a desire to help my chosen audience (Russians in the UK). Further, I knew I was very personable. I had met many Russian-speaking business acquaintances in London during my time as a solicitor, but I knew I needed to develop that network much more. I started attending networking events several times a week. I made sure I talked to as many people as I could, terrifying though it was. And, after some considerable time, I succeeded!

Gradually, I came to know several Russian-speaking professionals, estate agents, mortgage brokers and accountants quite well; many became good friends. They asked me whether I could help their clients, and I was happy to do so. That's how it all began in February 2012, in an organic, very gradual way, with my feet firmly on the ground – literally, with my feet on the streets of London, running from office to office and from meeting to meeting, telling everyone about our new law firm.

NOTE TO SELF

The beginning was painful and agonisingly slow. Although it cost almost nothing to set up a limited company in the UK, getting a licence for RSL-LAW to operate as a law firm took over six to eight months. Initially, I had no income – something you have to be prepared to go through as an entrepreneur. The little savings I did have quickly disappeared to pay our day-to-day living expenses. Once I jumped off the corporate wagon, I knew nobody would give me a pay cheque – it was up to me now to earn it. I did not have a regular job, and nor did I have a husband to look after us. It was simple – if I did not earn, we did not eat. I spent every waking hour focusing on getting the firm's name out there, meeting as many right people as possible, be they potential clients or introducers of potential clients. I once spent ten hours on end running around the streets of London, going from meeting to meeting, with people I had made appointments with earlier that week – mortgage brokers, accountants, estate agents, bankers.

Life was poor, times were tough, and it was normal for me to be in the office for fifteen to twenty hours each day with nothing to show at the end of the day. Yet I knew I was laying the foundations for the firm's future, and it was all beginning to make sense to me.

Larger city law firms dominated the market, however. Though often they had no Russian speakers, and if they did, they were usually junior people with little or no experience.

NOTE TO SELF

By 2015, the firm started employing people, and we started earning some money, but everything we made paid wages and bills, with next to nothing left at the end of every month. The workflow was good, but we were still not earning decent money. I asked myself, 'Why?' If everyone was busy, and instructions were coming in, why were we merely making ends meet? The answer was not clear to me then, but now I know what I should have done very early on, at the outset. I would have avoided sleepless nights and many years of financial struggle.

Regardless of the industry, for any business to be successful, you need to systemise it. You need to stop being the business. If it cannot operate without you, then you have merely created a job for yourself. The aim is to create a clear business structure with clear procedures and checklists for others to follow. The business should be able to operate without you, or at least without you working in the business full time. The role of the business owner is not day-to-day operations, but setting up and developing a structure that can be replicated with systems and procedures in place that can be followed by employees with the appropriate training.

Another problem we had back then in 2015, was that we positioned RSL-LAW as a legal practice offering services any other legal firm did. We didn't specialise in anything specifically, we offered general property law, family law and corporate law advice. Just like many law firms up and down the country. We were not 'specialists' in anything specific and no different from any other firm. You need to separate your business from the competition – find your niche and unique selling points. Your unique selling points can be anything, answering calls the same day or at weekends, meeting clients at their homes, or having late-night or weekend appointments. And, if you can find one, very specific unique selling point, an expertise and experience in something that no one, or only a few, offer, you will succeed over and above your expectations. If you do this well, your competitors will be left standing. The trick here is to be very focused. You should be able to name your unique selling point in less than twenty seconds or, even better, in less than ten. If you were to ask me, I could tell you ours in ten seconds: 'We are property solicitors in central London, specialising in buying properties for our clients, who wish to use foreign funds, money they earned outside the UK. We understand compliance for foreign buyers.' Time to identify yours …

Note to Self:

Don't start a business to give yourself a job. Being an entrepreneur is a full-time obsession. When you begin, you have to be prepared to live how no one wants to live so that you can eventually live how everyone would like to.

RSL-LAW Property Solicitors, based in central London, assisting property investors throughout the world

Just another day in the office...

There is no such thing as self-made, you are only as good as the team you build

Qualified solicitor and Managing Director of RSL LAW, Property Law Solicitors

9. BUILDING SOMETHING OF VALUE AND GETTING IT RIGHT

Markets were favourable when our legal practice opened in 2012. There had been a long standing trend of Russian-speaking business people coming to England to benefit from what the UK had to offer, such as business opportunities, good schooling and universities. Many were already successful in their home country but knew little to no English. The first problem they had was a problem with language – they could not achieve what they wanted because of difficulties communicating in English. More importantly, they could not understand how business is done here in the UK – and that is where we could help.

At the outset, my business experience was very limited and I relied on a cocktail of desire, personality, ambition and perseverance, so I could not capitalise upon demand. Then I started to earn good money as the firm's reputation grew and an increasing number of estate agents and businesspeople referred business to us. After the first ramp-up period, we reached a stage when we were firing on all cylinders, charging well for legal services. Having started in 2012, we initially had clients who did not live in the UK and who wished to come to the UK or send their children to school or university here. But from 2015 onwards, we began to have enquiries from clients already here, who had negative experiences with other law

NOTE TO SELF

firms whose solicitors could not understand their background, their language, or the documents these buyers provided.

Recent years have brought the unprecedented challenges of Brexit and Covid, which have put businesses on more of a survival footing. Even more recently, the war in Ukraine redefined how we now do business. It has been challenging, things have been uncertain, and we have been in unchartered waters, but perhaps turbulence is just the norm and the test of companies' sustainability and future viability. Now, the ultimate question is how to survive in the new world order that started before Brexit and is still taking formation today. How is survival possible when you have a very niche set of clients? I decided not to focus on clients' nationality but on the needs each client has, owing to their circumstances.

Many non-British residents need to transfer money from abroad to buy property in the UK using foreign banks. A transfer like this requires additional legal checks and approvals in the country before taking place. For that reason, we have developed specific advice to help with issues regarding the source of funds and devised a range of documents that any foreign bank would want to see for transactions to be approved; this has enabled us to spread our client base to include families from India, Turkey and Dubai.

Looking back at the history of my business, I created and sustained a job for myself and others for many years. Yes, I was the boss and the manager, but was I a leader? Was I entrepreneurial? No. I created a job for myself. I did it well, but the enterprise needed a long-term strategy, systemisation and much less reliance on me doing a job. For any entrepreneur, the result should be creating a business that they can keep or sell, should they want to, and that can successfully exist without a sole person being responsible for its success. I am now in a fortunate position – benefitting from years of experience, using the knowledge I have acquired to strengthen our legal practice. I also now have a full appreciation for the fact that, as an entrepreneur, you create and accept a particular lifestyle, and that lifestyle is unforgiving. You don't stop thinking about things when you go to bed. You can't simply switch off when Friday comes. You will always cancel birthdays or parties if the opportunity for a meeting to clinch a crucial piece of business comes along; this is your life, not merely your job.

And none of those sacrifices matter if you do not achieve financial success. It is the bottom line that matters. There is a balance between workload and profitability, and in the early days, I got that balance wrong. There was glamorous Tatiana with her law firm, like a swan, paddling harder and harder to keep still. It is too easy to become a slave to the business, to graft like a dervish without attaining adequate financial reward. I recognise that early on, I was hammering away almost for the sake of it, without enough focus on what revenue I was bringing in – or perhaps without sufficient understanding of how to take the business to the next level. If I had combined my success with clients, colleagues and

NOTE TO SELF

business partners with the three fundamentals for any enterprise I mentioned in the previous chapter, I would have avoided many sleepless nights.

There is enormous sacrifice in running a business. People rely on you. You are indispensable. You cannot let your clients down, and there are bills, salaries, and taxes to be paid. It is like an animal that becomes bigger than you, a monster constantly needs feeding. So, it is vital to get obsessed and fall in love with being an entrepreneur. I do not want my challenges to be less; I want to be better at dealing with them.

Note to Self:
If you want a quiet life and clear boundaries between your personal life and business, being an entrepreneur is not for you. Running a business, and being your own boss, is not for the faint-hearted. You are signing up for a lifetime of problem-solving, making uncomfortable decisions, and being on the receiving end of every possible complaint from clients, employees, and business partners – the buck stops with you! But you will also have fun along the way, networking, building business relationships, negotiating deals and getting things right. And if you are anything like me, once you get one business right, you will want more, and more and more, not even for the money but for the thrill of building something of value and getting it right!

My second home, the city of London

10. THE PRICE I'VE PAID FOR SUCCESS

I have learned so much from when I set out as that very naive, unsuspecting Russian girl in a Moscow airport. But despite all the victories I've had along the way, big and small, the price for being who I am today and running several businesses for eleven years has been very high.

Being on my own during those years has been the most challenging. Studying and working so hard meant that I could not be there for my son when he was growing up, and I feel I missed his childhood and was not the support he needed during his formative years. We were surviving, so I had no choice. I provided the necessities – a roof over our heads and food to eat – but I did not have the sufficient life experience or personal maturity to give the moral or mental guidance a young boy needed. Partly it was the reality of being a single mother – I was the mum and the dad. I was always so stressed, barely functioning, making sure my son was at school on time, that I was in the office, and that we had enough money to pay rent, buy food and pay the bills. The bigger picture eluded me. I felt forever guilty not being a full-time mum that I overcompensated with love and forgiveness when, at times, the young boy needed structure and guidance.

NOTE TO SELF

We have only seen his father once in all this time. He appeared again one day when we were in our miserable basement flat. Amidst the rhythm of us walking 25 minutes to the nearest supermarket because we had no car, of taking my son to the park to play football at the weekends as some semblance of normality, of darting between university and school, H suddenly appeared on our doorstep one evening. I do not know how he found me – he had never offered any help of any sort over the years – but there he was, the absent father with an Action Man toy in his hand as a token gesture to my son, who had no idea who 'that man' was. Having left us plunged into total silence and desertion, H stood there, uttering the feeble words, 'Stuff happened, and I needed to go away.'

Why had he come? He wanted a divorce. He found us and appeared on our doorstep because he wanted a divorce. To this day, the female mind fascinates me – or mine does, in any case. Because I loved him once, despite what he put us through, I remember beginning to feel sorry for him as he told me how tough his life had been in the past few years. I felt sorry for him, not myself, destitute and emotionally broken for years. I did not answer him at the time – I was too shocked at seeing him after all this time. I did not even ask him 'Why?' or 'How do you sleep at night?' or 'How was it possible what happened?' Instead, we had the most meaningless conversation about nothing. It lasted ten minutes. Then he left and froze us out again, sending not a word nor a penny. He had contributed nothing over the years, and having no permanent address made it impossible for me even to try to get some help from him through official channels.

A year or so later, I divorced him unilaterally with the help of legal aid and on the grounds of abandonment, but basically, he got away with what he had done. The devastating effects of abandonment stayed with my son and me for years. We dealt with it in different ways, both separately and together. I will never fully recover; he truly broke my heart. I will always have scars, but I am a better person for it. I am what I am today because I had to survive, sacrifice and suffer real grief. My son, I am sure, felt like a lost soul at times, trying to understand life as he knew it by himself whilst I was straggling to provide. The result was that for most of the earlier years, we were bouncing off each other's frustration, with nobody else to share the strain, and as a result, we got caught in a cycle of not listening to or understanding one another and often breaking each other's hearts. We were both in search of support and love, but I was too stressed to see what mattered, and my son was too young to understand how much, just how much, I needed support and understanding.

After all this, I am thankful that something went right and that I have a kind, loyal, loving son. Despite the upheaval, he put what happened to us behind him, grew up and matured into an incredible human being. We have a brilliant relationship now – we can discuss anything, there is no more anger or blame, and he is quite simply my best friend. We have both grown up and migrated beyond the difficulties of earlier years. He recognises how hard I had to try to keep us afloat and the sacrifices I made, whilst I can now appreciate how confusing life was for him and how much he craved my time, love and guidance.

Note to Self:
For self-preservation and our emotional comfort, we blame others, unfortunate circumstances, a bad start in life, bad luck, or anything else we can think of as a reason why we are what we are, why we behave a certain way, or to explain our lot in life. It's not wrong; it is just who we are. It's human nature. The search for someone or something to blame is always successful.
Understanding that everything in your life begins with only you and the decisions you make is one of the most important assets you can have. Continuing to be sad or bitter, blaming the past for present circumstances, is to continue living as a victim of those circumstances. Draw the line, create your own possibilities, change your environment, and decide to have the life you want, the life you think you deserve.

11. WHAT NEXT, TATIANA?

What a journey it has been – becoming a woman, a mum, an entrepreneur, driven by my English experiences and the love I had from my parents, who always taught me to keep moving and to survive and better myself. I have learned much in the last decade – about business, relationships, struggles and success. And yet, the one lesson I wish I had realised much earlier in life is financial intelligence. Or, in other words – the truth about money.

I have learned throughout my journey that you will never have it all if you believe in that old-fashioned and mistaken premise that the harder you try, the more successful you become. The hardest-working people are often the poorest. Financial intelligence is how to work smart, but not necessarily hard. For years, I lacked financial intelligence and followed the accepted path. I enjoyed university very much, and it gave me an entirely different perspective on life in general, but it did not give me any financial education – financial intelligence, making money work for me instead of working hard for my money. It is instilled in us from a very young age to get good marks at school, go to university, get a degree, get a good job, be a good employee and try hard; then, after a few years, you will gain recognition, be promoted and find happiness: a family, a mortgage, credit cards. It took me eight years to qualify as an English solicitor, and at the

NOTE TO SELF

end of it, I was overstressed, unhappy, unfulfilled and a guilty parent.

The fear of the unknown, being left without a guaranteed pay cheque, prolonged my suffering for another few years. Then, even with the legal practice, the lack of a good mentor and being inexperienced myself meant that it took a long time to get where we needed to be. We offered good service, earned money, but we were limited in our growth and expansion because the business relied on one person and one person only, me. I was the rainmaker and the manager, and I was providing legal advice and secretarial support and posting letters and doing millions of other tasks in a day. I was doing a job, I did it well, but most of my time was taken up by day-to-day operations, leaving no time for developing income-generating strategies, expanding our professional network, and strengthening our position and branding in the market. If you asked me then to name our unique selling point in less than twenty seconds, I would have been lost, and probably waffled on about how great our client care is (hmmm, should be given) or how responsive we are, again, hardly differentiates one law firm from another. I simply did not know why RSL-LAW was different from any other legal practice in the country. I do now! Now, finally, I enjoy my business life to the full. I have set up several more businesses since our law firm – all relating to real estate. As I said, all great journeys start from the first step.

NOTE TO SELF

So, what is next for me? Just me – not as a lawyer, businesswoman or entrepreneur. The answer is living - just living how I want to live, surrounded only by those people who make me happy and doing only the jobs I choose to do. I have finally found myself and know who I am. The anger has gone. I drew the line, learned to forgive, and wasted no time being a victim or angry.

Putting my story on paper shows me that I have come out the other side of those terrible experiences and that I am OK. This book will end my ever feeling like a victim again.

Note to Self:
Happiness is not a goal; it's a process. Stop thinking you will be happy as soon as you get that new job, buy that house, or save for that holiday. Choose to be contented every single day. Surround yourself only with positive energy. If someone in your life is not rooting for you, doubting your journey, or making you feel unhappy, then walk away and let them be. You deserve to have the best journey called 'life'.
And most importantly, spread love – make sure everyone who comes into your life with love is happier for knowing you, as it will all come right back to you.

Another viewing of a stunning farm house. Is this my next development project?

The Samuel Leeds Property Academy: winning the Peoples' Choice Award: the Academy Member of the Year, October 2022

Presenting at the Property event; sharing my journey from a start-up to a successful six figure income business

DEDICATION

To Ludmila, in loving memory, Victor, with enormous gratitude, and my son for giving my life meaning. I dedicate my story to my family. Without their influence, unconditional love and total acceptance of me with all my victories and challenges, I truly believe I would not have survived.

My parents gave me the strength to better myself, to keep going and compete. Like me, my mother was a hardworking woman, often juggling three or four jobs to provide for us. What's more, she was the shining light at any party – outrageous, extroverted and always happy, thanks to the energy she had and that I shared.

My father was always there for me – creative, reading me poetry, always at my level when I was a child. He gave me a thirst for education and for improving myself. Moments with him are encapsulated in my memory – riding on the back of his bike on endless rides through woods and parks, me singing Russian songs with gay abandon to the delight of passers-by, my arms flung around his waist. That's my father.

My son has held me together without knowing it. Being responsible for him kept me going even at the most challenging times and on the gloomiest evenings. I only had to

NOTE TO SELF

wake up to see this little boy looking at me expectantly, waiting to be fed, hoping to go to the park, to know that I could not possibly allow myself to fall apart. He has saved me and been my rock without knowing it. He has allowed me to grow up as a person, together with him.

What seems to us as bitter trials are often blessings in disguise.
— Oscar Wilde

You didn't teach me how to be a good person, you showed me instead! RIP

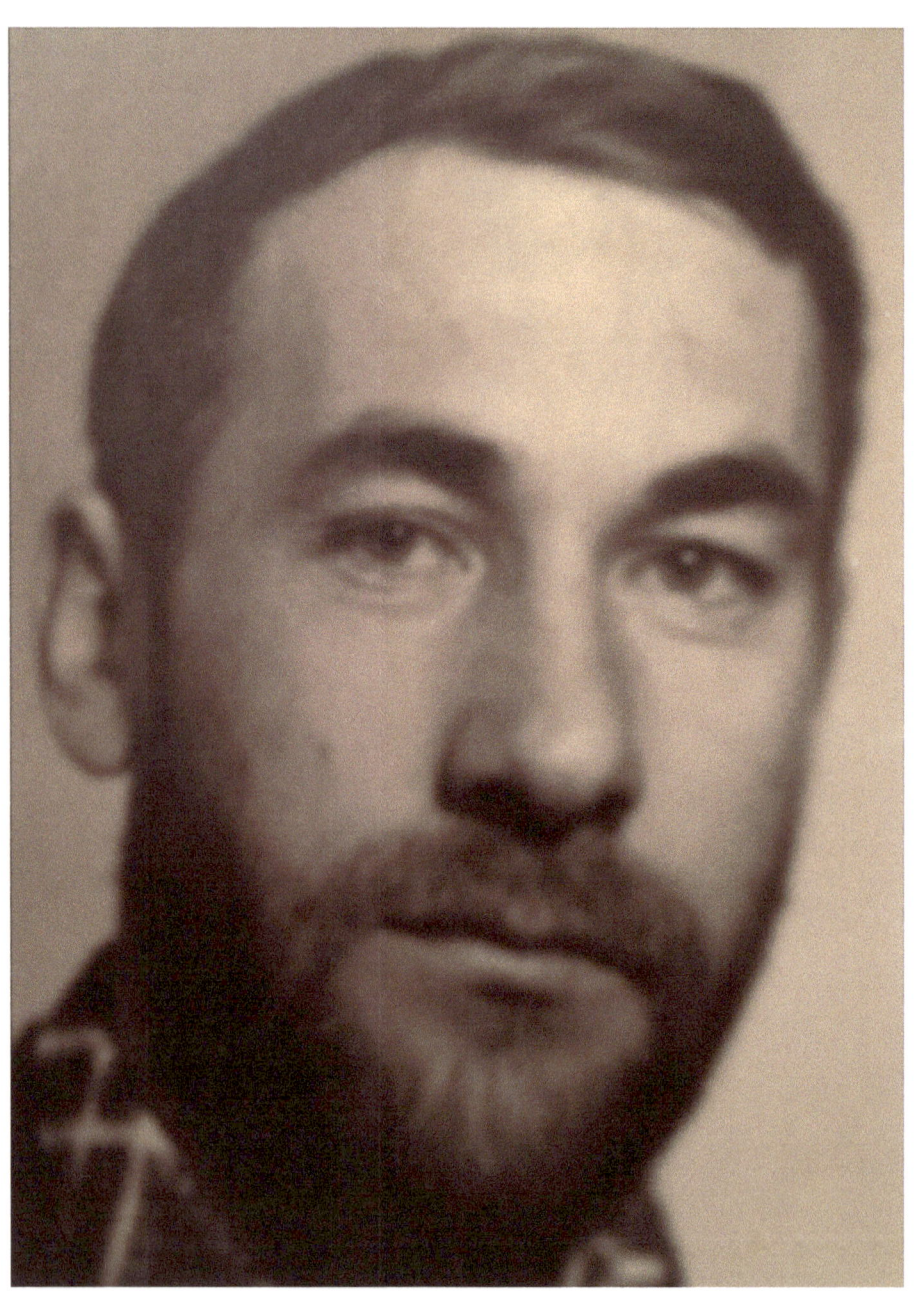

Dad, my best friend who has always been there, love you papa

Papa! I am your 'little girl' forever

My biggest achievement - an amazing young man who I am very proud of!

Looking forward to the next chapter in my life...

Hammersmith Recording Studios, London - recording of Homeless Single Mum To Six-Figure Income in progress

www.ingramcontent.com/pod-product-compliance
Lightning Source LLC
Chambersburg PA
CBHW042130100526
44587CB00026B/4237